© 2015 Sunny Dawn Johnston Productions | www.sunnydawnjohnston.com/mandalas

Copyright © 2015

By Sunny Dawn Johnston

All rights reserved, including the right to reproduce this work in any form whatsoever, without permission in writing from the publisher.

Cover Art by Artist Lori Farrell

Mandala Artwork by Artist Lori Farrell

Doodle Artwork by Artist Staci Mitchell Randall

Cover Design and Layout by Graphic Designer Kris Voelker

Formatted for Print by Shanda Trofe

For permission requests, write to the publisher:

Sunny Dawn Johnston Productions

4640 W. Redfield Road

Glendale, AZ 85306

www.sunnydawnjohnston.com

ISBN: 978-0979811944

Printed on acid-free paper in the United States

This book is dedicated to

the creative spirit

within each and every one of us!

~ *Sunny Dawn Johnston*

Contents

What is a Doodle?..1

What is a Dala (Mandala)?...1

Benefits of Coloring...2

Doodles & Dalas Coloring Tips..3

    Color Symbolism Chart..3

    Color Mediums..4

    Techniques for Coloring..5

The Artist's Perspectives...7

    Healing with Doodles..7

    Healing with Mandalas..8

Biographies..9

Section 1 – Doodles...**13**

Section 2 – Dalas..**55**

What is a Doodle?

A doodle is a simple drawing that can have real meaning, or may just be abstract shapes. Popular kinds of doodles include cartoons and geometric shapes, patterns, designs and textures. Typical examples of doodling are found in notebooks - often in the margins - drawn by people during meetings, lectures or telephone conversations. Many American Presidents (including Thomas Jefferson, Ronald Reagan and Bill Clinton) have been known to doodle during meetings. Some doodles have even been found in the notebooks of Leonardo da Vinci.

Doodling is meant to be spontaneous, which means your brain isn't focused on the final design, but is simply present in the moment of the creation. **Doodles** are created with an intention to express oneself with no rules or guidelines ... to just go with the flow and create outside-the-box. Creating and coloring doodles can help you release the worry of having things looks perfect, and instead, just allow it to BE ... Perfection in the imperfection. Coloring **Doodles** will help you to focus your energy in a healthy way, releasing the fear and worry, at least for those moments of time that are spent coloring.

Doodling gets the neurons to fire and expands the mind. According to a study published in the scientific journal *Applied Cognitive Psychology*, doodling can aid a person's memory by freeing up short and long-term memory, improve content retention and increase attention span. It can also produce creative insight and relieve stress. Give your mind a break. The human mind is very habit forming. To break the habit of worry, stress and anxiety, you have to think in an unfamiliar way—a visual way. Therefore, coloring in your ***Doodles & Dalas Coloring Book*** can be the beginning of retraining your brain.

What is a Dala (Mandala)?

A mandala is a design which represents the Universe and is used as a focal point of meditation; a collection point for Universal Forces. The term mandala is of Sanskrit origin meaning circle. Mandalas are usually created using repetitive patterns.

People of all faiths and beliefs use mandalas as a spiritual guidance tool to help them clear their minds, focus, and establish sacred space to pave the way for meditation, inner peace and internal awareness.

The act of coloring the mandala design can be therapeutic by bringing into light a sense of well-being, and finding balance. Focusing on a task, letting your thoughts wander and shutting out stressors, leads to a clear and healthy mind, body and soul.

Benefits of Coloring

You **do not** have to be an artist to color **Doodles and Dalas**. You only need to create the time and space to tap into the energy within and allow yourself to release any energy that is for your highest good. Coloring as guided without a focus on the end result makes the experience a personal and healing journey. There is no **right or wrong way,** just use your own guidance and intuition.

Some of the benefits of coloring *Doodles & Dalas***:**

- Concentration
- Focus
- Clarity
- Meditation
- Increased Intuition
- Pain Relief
- Emotional Healing
- Stress Reduction
- Release Addiction
- Release Anxiety
- Mental Sharpness
- Mindfulness

Choose a design that speaks to your inner needs at the present moment. This book is not to be done in any particular order, but instead as guided. Different colors represent many different feelings and emotions (see the list on the color sheet). Once you choose a design, color the design based on how you are feeling, what you are presently working on personally, and what comes to you naturally. You may want to do your coloring first thing in the morning to start your day on a relaxed and positive note as part of your meditation practice. Or in the evening just before bedtime to release the thought energy of the day and promote a relaxed sense of well-being for deeper and healthier sleep.

Doodles & Dalas Coloring Tips

Color is EVERYWHERE! Take a moment to look around you ... notice all the colors in your surroundings. The color palette is endless! Color makes us feel many things – excitement, joy and serenity, to name a few. It helps us to express our emotions, even the negative ones, in fun and healthy ways.

Doodles & Dalas Coloring Book is full of original, detailed designs and patterns for you to use in a variety of different ways. As you color these beautiful designs you will find yourself focused, centered, and at peace. The images are printed on 8.5" x 11" high quality paper so you'll have plenty of space to express your creativity. After you are finished, you'll have lovely works of art, ready to hang on the wall and inspire continued healing.

Color Symbolism Chart:

Red: Excitement, energy, passion, love, desire, speed, strength, power, heat, aggression, danger, fire, blood, war, violence, all things intense and passionate.

Pink symbolizes love and romance, caring, tenderness, acceptance and calm.

Beige and ivory symbolize unification. Ivory symbolizes quiet and pleasantness. **Beige** symbolizes calm and simplicity.

Yellow signifies joy, happiness, betrayal, optimism, idealism, imagination, hope, sunshine, summer, gold, philosophy, dishonesty, cowardice, jealousy, covetousness, deceit, illness, hazard and friendship.

Dark Blue symbolizes integrity, knowledge, power, and seriousness.

Blue: Peace, tranquility, cold, calm, stability, harmony, unity, trust, truth, confidence, conservatism, security, cleanliness, order, loyalty, sky, water, technology, depression, appetite suppressant.

Turquoise symbolizes calm. **Teal** symbolizes sophistication. **Aquamarine** symbolizes water. **Lighter turquoise** has a feminine appeal.

Purple: Royalty, nobility, spirituality, ceremony, mysterious, transformation, wisdom, enlightenment, cruelty, honor, arrogance, mourning, temperance.

Lavender symbolizes femininity, grace and elegance.

Orange: Energy, balance, enthusiasm, warmth, vibrant, expansive, flamboyant, demanding of attention.

Green: Nature, environment, healthy, good luck, renewal, youth, spring, generosity, fertility, jealousy, service, inexperience, envy, misfortune, vigor.

Brown: Earth, stability, hearth, home, outdoors, reliability, comfort, endurance, simplicity, and comfort.

Gray: Security, reliability, intelligence, staid, modesty, dignity, maturity, solid, conservative, practical, old age, sadness, boring. **Silver** symbolizes calm.

White: Reverence, purity, birth, simplicity, cleanliness, peace, humility, precision, innocence, youth, winter, snow, good, sterility, cold, clinical.

Black: Power, sexuality, sophistication, formality, elegance, wealth, mystery, fear, evil, unhappiness, depth, style, sadness, remorse, anger, anonymity, underground, good technical color, mourning, death, austerity, detachment.

Color Mediums:

There are many types of mediums you can use to color an image: crayons, colored pencils, colored chalk, markers to name a few. If you are just starting out, your supplies do not need to be artist quality, expensive tools. Grab a simple set of colored pencils, crayons or markers at your local drugstore just to get the feel of it. Once you have mastered a few techniques, you may want to buy artist quality tools – you will find that the better the quality, the better the result. Below are listed a few suggested brands as examples.

CRAYONS
Crayons are an inexpensive product and they come a wide variety of colors. You can apply different colored crayons in layers, one over the other to create an effect. They are wax based and easy to apply; however, they are not blendable in nature.

COLORED PENCILS
Strongly suggested for beginners. Colored pencils come in a wide variety of colors. There are many brands on the market to choose from that vary in price based on the quality and pigment in the colored lead. Some are wax based and some are oil based. All are blendable and easy to shade with and layer colors. Colored pencil can be blended with a stump (cardboard or cotton rolled into a stick with a point – available at your local craft store in the drawing section). They can also be blended with a non-color blender marker.

NOTE: Use a separate pencil sharpener for your colored pencils that has not been used for a regular graphite lead pencil; otherwise, the lead will adhere to the pencil and you will get pencil smudges mixed in with your color. Best suggestion is to purchase a separate sharpener and label it "colored pencils only".

COLORED CHALK
Colored chalk comes in a palette with many colors to choose from. They come in squares or sticks. The fun thing about chalk is they are easy to blend and layer colors. They can be applied with a Q-tip, cosmetic sponge, paint brush, or stump. The easiest applicator is a cosmetic Q-tip purchased at your local drug store – they have a tip that is pointed and a tip that is round. With chalk, you simply swipe across the chalk and then apply it to the paper in a tight circular motion. The chalk becomes embedded into the fine grooves of the paper. Excess chalk can be lightly brushed away or blow on the paper to remove excess chalk dust. The result is very soft, subtle and lovely.

MARKERS
IMPORTANT: If you use markers, please use the included protection page as well as a piece of cardboard under the page you are coloring to protect the following pages. There are many colored marker brands on the market to choose from as well and costs vary. The easiest to use are the brush tip markers, but the fine and bullet tip markers work as well. You will find what works best for you as you try different products.

MIXED MEDIA
Mixed media is the use of several different types of media on one piece of artwork, such as markers, colored pencils and chalk – all used to create different effects on one artwork design.

Techniques for Coloring:

It is best to start with the lightest shade of a color and add more color to it. Remember, if you color something in with a dark color, it usually cannot be changed. Dark colors are beautiful and fun to use, but if you want to layer color, you need to start light and add more color to work up to a brighter shade.

Shading is done by applying a light layer of color and then going back into the corners, edges or places where you know would be farthest away and add more color. Blend as you go along. You can layer several different colors on top of each other to make new colors! The possibilities are endless!

When coloring a mandala – choose the colors that best describe how you are feeling in the moment. Let the design help you express your inner feelings ... which will help you release them ... beginning the healing process. It is recommended to work from the center outward to obtain a feeling of releasing your inner spirit.

Ready! Set! Go!

Let your creativity flow! The fun part about art is there is no RIGHT or WRONG way to design it – if you open your mind to what you are feeling and let that energy flow into your work – a masterpiece will be created! And what a wonderful feeling to look down at your artwork and know if came from within YOU! Have fun! And if you make a mistake – don't stress! Most mistakes become something even better. When it comes to art – there are no mistakes! My hope is that you will enjoy coloring these designs and let your inner spirit sing!

~ Sunny Dawn Johnston

Healing with Doodles

An Artist's Story by Doodle Artist Staci Mitchell Randall

Growing up, art was one of my favorite classes. Math and English simply were not my subjects. I would doodle, draw, write and create craft projects in my spare time. Shy and introverted, art became a way for me to express my feelings and emotions. It was very much an outlet for me. I always thought it would be fun to be an artist, but I felt I needed more talent than what I had – so I never pursued it any further... it was just a hobby.

Roaming through Pinterest one day, I came across some doodles. They were beautiful works of art. I was Inspired. I had always been a doodler in some respects, but never really saw it this way. I found myself looking at different doodles and watching video's about doodling. I bought drawing paper and pens and I began doodling myself. I purchased a book that had different doodle patterns in it and practiced drawing them. I doodled every day. As someone that has suffered with anxiety for as long as I can remember, it calmed me down, centered me and brought me peace of mind. It was fun and lighthearted for me too.

But, when my husband was diagnosed with cancer, I relied on it in a completely different way. I had a lot of time to think during all of the hospital visits while he was having tests and procedures done. I realized that wasn't the best place for me to be as I had a lot of fear. So, I doodled. I would doodle while in the waiting rooms. I could get out of my head and the world was shut out while I doodled. It was very calming. My pen just flowed with a serene and pleasant feel along the paper. I couldn't stop doodling. I needed it. I found this hobby very enjoyable, therapeutic, and simple. Soon I was able to understand, it wasn't just a hobby, but that it helped me be able to process the experience with my husband's cancer in a much healthier and grounded way.

My journey with my husband's cancer treatments continue ... and I keep doodling on. I was never very good with words, either on paper or verbally. Words just never felt like they flowed. However, when I am doodling, I can express myself. I can release the anxiety and fear and everything feels alright.

~ **Staci Mitchell Randall**

Healing with Mandalas

An Artist's Story by Mandala Artist Lori Farrell

I injured my back in an accident which lead to me having three surgeries. I had to walk with a walker and learn to do things differently. The pain in my back was excruciating. After the last surgery, I began experiencing pain in my feet. When I woke in recovery, I could hear myself screaming! I had unbearable pain in the heels of my feet! I thought they had cut my feet for some reason during surgery and my groggy, post-anesthetic head could not make sense of it. For about six months, I could barely walk because any pressure to my heels was like someone driving railroad spikes into the soles of my feet. In addition, I did not have the motor capability of standing or walking on my toes any longer from the back injury. Then, mysterious symptoms began to occur – my ankle would swell and turn purple, blue and red and my foot felt like it was on fire one minute and freezing the next. I could not handle even the slightest thing touching my foot, such as shoes, socks, or even the sheet on the bed.

I was diagnosed with RSD/CRPS (now known as Chronic Regional Pain Syndrome). Presently, there is no cure for this disease. The treatment is merely "pain management". My doctors referred me to a pain management specialist. I underwent the typical treatments: injections, medications, physical therapy, and the list goes on. I am a sensitive person, both emotionally and physically. I cannot take medications without suffering all the side effects. One day, I was at an appointment with my pain management doctor to discuss the very few remaining options left… it was then that she recommended Art Therapy as a sort-of biofeedback type approach to my pain. Having always loved arts, crafts, and anything artistic, I was excited to explore this approach. This began my journey into the love of drawing and coloring mandalas.

Most days are spent tipped back in my electric recliner, CREATING! Drawing and coloring mandalas has become my passion. I get lost in the repetitive design work and before I know it, hours have passed. And I am living proof that what heals the mind, heals the body! When I lose myself in this repetitive, almost tedious action, I am thinking about what I am creating, and therefore, not focusing on the pain in my body. I love to see my designs "come to life" as they are being created layer by layer, circle by circle. This has healed my inner spirit as well, by giving me a positive focus for the day and a sense of accomplishment when I see my finished artwork. I am grateful to my doctor who recommended this – it has changed my life. I still have pain on a daily basis, but I simply shift my mind into working on a mandala design and LIFE IS GOOD!

~ Lori Farrell

For more information about RSD please go to: http://www.rsdhope.org/what-is-crps.html

Biographies

Sunny Dawn Johnston – Creator

Sunny Dawn Johnston is an Inspirational Speaker, Spiritual Teacher and Psychic Medium. She is the best-selling author of *The Love Never Ends* and *Invoking the Archangels*. Sunny is the founder of Sunlight Alliance Healing Center, a spiritual healing center for people of like-minds and hearts to come together to expand, grow and heal. She lives in sunny Arizona and is very active in her community outreach programs. Visit her website at www.sunnydawnjohnston.com

Kris Voelker – Book Designer

Kris Voelker is the founder of Kris Voelker Designs LLC, a graphic/multimedia/web design business. She specialized in the self-help spiritual industry and has created designs for Sunny Dawn Johnston, James Van Praagh, Lisa Williams, Mishka Productions, Britain's best-loved psychic Sally Morgan, and many more. Her skillset is vast and she has won numerous awards for her design work. She enjoys working with her clients from an intuitive center. On any given day, you will most likely find her next to a piece of technology. See her work at krisvoelkerdesigns.com

Biographies

Staci Mitchell Randall – Artist

Staci Mitchell Randall has always loved to do arts and crafts as a hobby. Anything and everything craft – she loves. She grew up in Kamas, a tiny town near the mountains of Park City, Utah. After graduating with her Bachelors in Psychology, she became a para educator and works as a special education teacher in a high school setting. Her career is challenging and a blessing, all at the same time. Doodling became not only a creative outlet for her, but also a way of healing through her own personal and professional challenges.

Staci lives in Ogden, Utah with her husband Steve, cat Oscar and dog Spike. She enjoys expressing herself through creative projects such as remodeling, scrapbooking, journaling, woodworking, and most of all doodling. For more information about Staci or to contact her directly, please email her at 444.skeetr@gmail.com

Lori Farrell – Artist

Lori Farrell is a long-time crafter and artist. She grew up in an artistic family, taking after her great-grandfather who loved to draw realistic landscapes and animals. She worked as an insurance adjuster and taught classes at a local scrapbooking store until injured in an accident. She now spends her time creating unique pet portraits and custom drawings. Lori has a great love of nature, animals, and a connection with dragonflies!

Lori has experienced adversity and personal growth. She has had confirmation of her guardian angel on an MRI imaging study of her back injury, shocking even the doctor who witnessed it! She resides in Goodyear, AZ with her beloved pets and enjoys her passion for drawing and creating works of art. Check out her designs at www.etsy.com/shop/TwistedArtDesigns or twistedartdesigns444@gmail.com

IMPORTANT:

Insert a cardboard divider page when coloring with markers to protect bleed through.

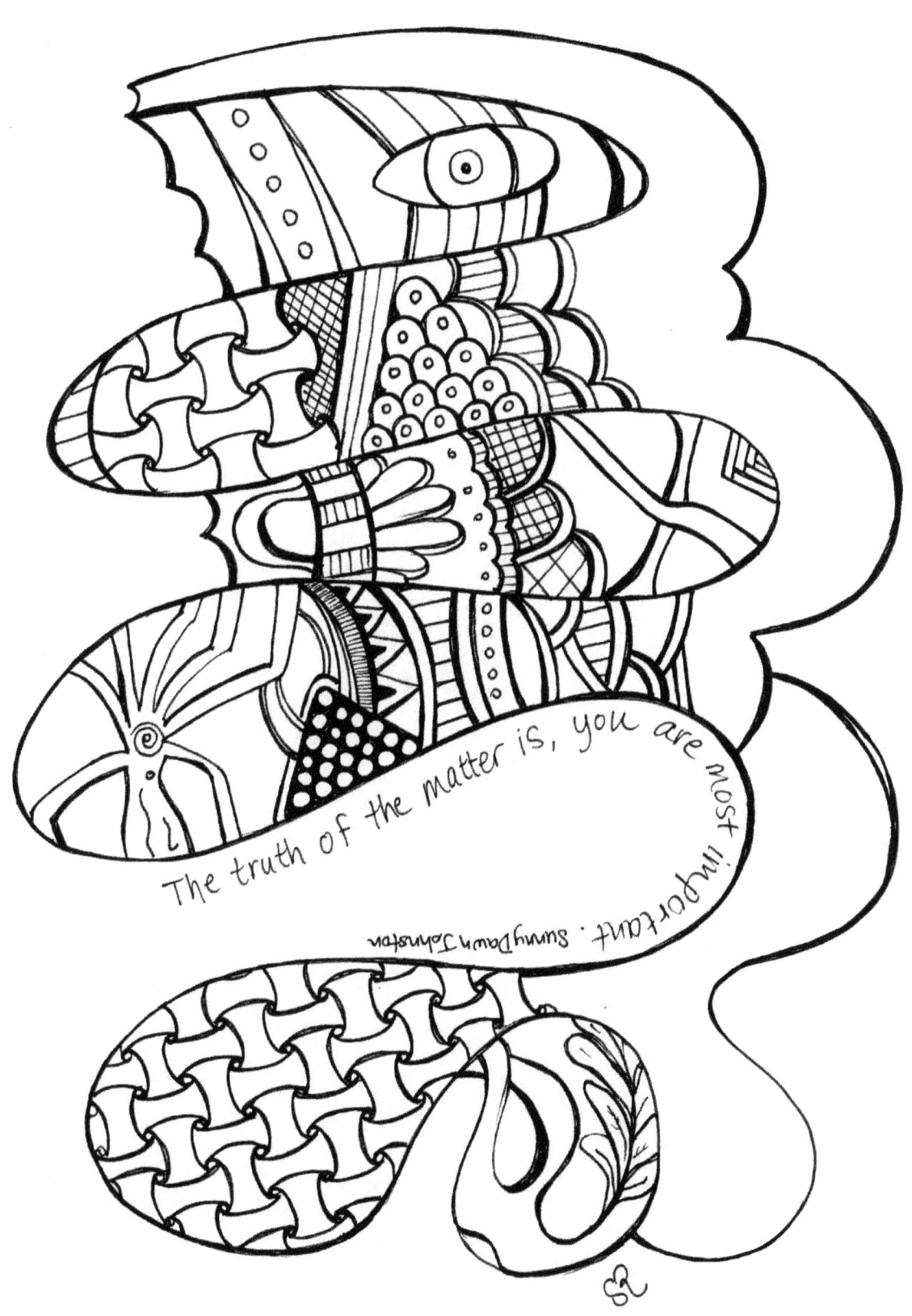

BLUE

If you've enjoyed this coloring book, please check out:

Healing Mandalas Coloring Book

www.ingramcontent.com/pod-product-compliance
Lightning Source LLC
Chambersburg PA
CBHW080446110426
42743CB00016B/3298